ARiL-4.2/p

W9-CMZ-133

North Carolina

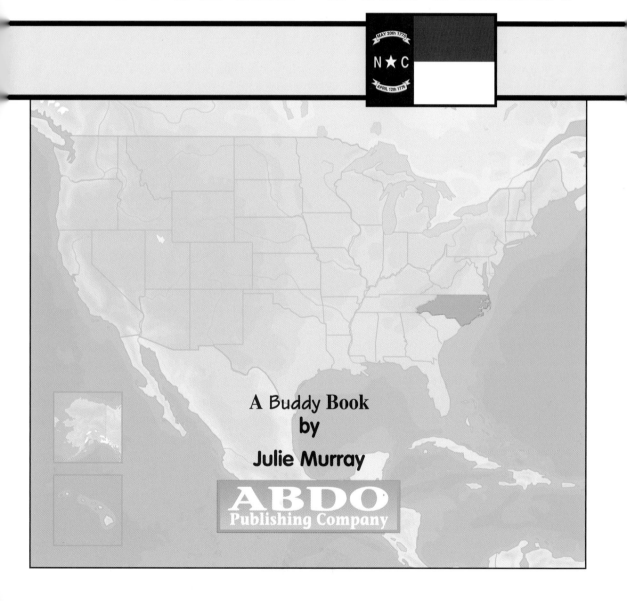

A Buddy Book
by
Julie Murray

ABDO
Publishing Company

VISIT US AT

www.abdopub.com

Published by ABDO Publishing Company, 4940 Viking Drive, Edina, Minnesota 55435.

Printed in the United States.

Edited by: Sarah Tieck
Contributing Editor: Michael P. Goecke
Graphic Design: Deb Coldiron, Maria Hosley
Image Research: Sarah Tieck
Photographs: Clipart.com, Comstock, Getty Images, Library of Congress, One Mile Up, Photodisc Photos.com

Library of Congress Cataloging-in-Publication Data

Murray, Julie, 1969-
  North Carolina / Julie Murray.
    p. cm. — (The United States)
  Includes bibliographical references and index.
  ISBN 1-59197-692-8
    1. North Carolina—Juvenile literature. I. Title.

F254.3.M87 2005
975.6—dc22

                                    2005045238

Table Of Contents

A Snapshot Of North Carolina

When people think of North Carolina, they think of its products. North Carolina has more tobacco farms than any other state in the United States. Also, it is known for making textiles and wooden furniture.

A tobacco farm in North Carolina.

There are 50 states in the United States. Every state is different. Every state has an official nickname. North Carolina is known as the "Tar Heel State." This is because North Carolina used to produce tar.

During one of the American Civil War battles, some of the Confederate soldiers left before the battle was over. North Carolina's soldiers had to fight alone. They said they would put tar on the heels of other soldiers next time. This would make them stick around for the battle.

North Carolina was one of the 13 colonies. Some believe it was the first colony to say that it was ready to be free from England's rule.

North Carolina became the 12th state on November 21, 1789. Today, it is the 28th-largest state in the United States. It has 52,672 square miles (136,420 sq km) of land. North Carolina is home to 8,049,313 people.

North Carolina has scenic landscapes.

Where Is North Carolina?

There are four parts of the United States. Each part is called a region. Each region is in a different area of the country. The United States Census Bureau says the four regions are the Northeast, the South, the Midwest, and the West.

Four Regions of the United States of America

ALASKA

WASHINGTON

OREGON

MONTANA

IDAHO

NORTH DAKOTA

MINNESOTA

WISCONSIN

MICHIGAN

VERMONT

MAINE

NEW HAMPSHIRE

MASSACHUSETTS

NEW YORK

RHODE ISLAND

CONNECTICUT

WYOMING

SOUTH DAKOTA

IOWA

PENNSYLVANIA

NEW JERSEY

NEVADA

UTAH

NEBRASKA

ILLINOIS

INDIANA

OHIO

DELAWARE

Washington D.C.

MARYLAND

WEST VIRGINIA

VIRGINIA

CALIFORNIA

COLORADO

KANSAS

MISSOURI

KENTUCKY

NORTH CAROLINA

TENNESSEE

SOUTH CAROLINA

ARIZONA

NEW MEXICO

OKLAHOMA

ARKANSAS

MISSISSIPPI

ALABAMA

GEORGIA

TEXAS

LOUISIANA

FLORIDA

HAWAII

West   Midwest   South   Northeast

The weather is cool in North Carolina's mountains.

North Carolina is in the South region of the United States. Generally, the state has mild weather throughout the year. It is usually warmer near the coast and cooler in the mountains. Sometimes it gets cold enough to snow during the winter months in North Carolina.

North Carolina is bordered by four other states and a body of water. Virginia is to the north. Tennessee is to the west. Georgia and South Carolina are to the south. The Atlantic Ocean is east.

North Carolina

State abbreviation: NC

State nickname: Tar Heel State

State capital: Raleigh

State motto: *Esse quam videri* (Latin for "To Be, Rather Than To Seem")

Statehood: November 21, 1789, 12th state

Population: 8,049,313, ranks 11th

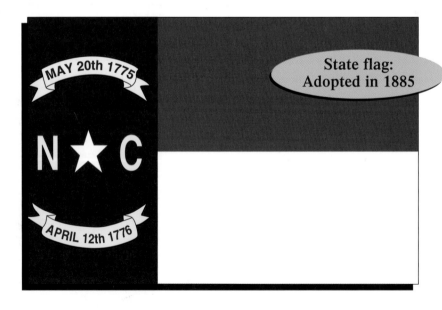

State flag: Adopted in 1885

Land area: 52,672 square miles (136,420 sq km), ranks 28th

State song: "The Old North State"

State government: Three branches: legislative, executive, and judicial

Average July temperature: 70°F (21°C)

Average January temperature: 41°F (5°C)

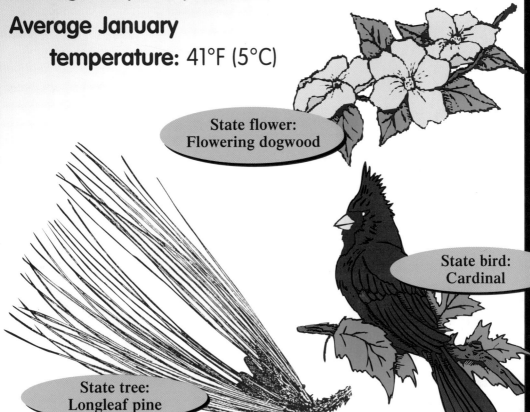

State flower:
Flowering dogwood

State bird:
Cardinal

State tree:
Longleaf pine

Cities And The Capital

Raleigh is the capital city of North Carolina. It is also the second-largest city in the state. Raleigh became the state capital in 1792. Raleigh is close to the cities of Durham and Chapel Hill. They form one metropolitan area.

Research Triangle Park is a triangle-shaped area that is home to more than 100 research and development companies. It is located in Raleigh, Durham, and Chapel Hill.

Charlotte is North Carolina's largest city. It is a transportation center for the southeastern part of the United States. Charlotte is also known as a financial center for the United States. Many banks are located there.

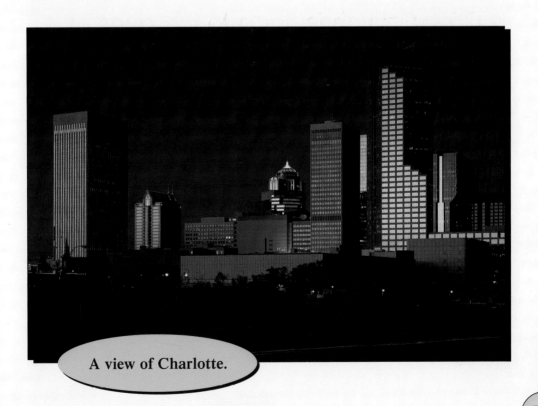

A view of Charlotte.

Famous Citizens

John Coltrane (1926–1967)

John Coltrane was born in Hamlet in 1926. He grew up in High Point. Coltrane was a famous jazz artist who played the saxophone. He played with other famous jazz musicians such as Dizzy Gillespie and Miles Davis. He also played on his own. One of his most popular songs was "My Favorite Things."

John Coltrane

Famous Citizens

Andrew Johnson (1808–1875)

Andrew Johnson was born in Raleigh in 1808. He was the 17th president of the United States. Johnson was vice president under President Abraham Lincoln. When Lincoln was shot and killed in 1865, Johnson became the president. Johnson served as president from 1865 to 1869. He was the first president to be impeached.

Andrew Johnson

The Lost Colony

Roanoke Island is the site of a 418-year-old mystery.

Roanoke Island is located off the coast of North Carolina. In May 1587, Sir Walter Raleigh formed a colony there. This colony was one of the first English colonies in America. It was home to 117 settlers. Men, women, and children lived there.

Sir Walter Raleigh

Sir Walter Raleigh trades items with the
Native Americans in North Carolina.

Some people say these settlers made friends with the Croatoan Native Americans. They believe Croatoans helped the settlers get food and supplies. But, disagreements caused problems between the English settlers and the Native Americans. They say that the settlers were struggling to survive.

This drawing is by John White. It shows Native Americans in North Carolina.

John White was the governor of the colony. He decided to go to England for food and supplies to help the settlers. He sailed for England in August 1587. While he was there, a war started between England and Spain. White could not return to Roanoke Island until the war ended.

When White returned in 1590, all of the settlers were gone. The word "Croatoan" was carved into a tree. Some people say the settlers went to live with the Croatoans. But, no one knows what happened to the settlers of Roanoke Island. This is why it is sometimes called "The Lost Colony."

Cape Hatteras National Seashore

Cape Hatteras National Seashore.

Cape Hatteras National Seashore stretches for more than 70 miles (113 km). It is a group of islands off the coast of North Carolina. It became the first national seashore in the United States in 1953.

The water around Cape Hatteras is dangerous for ships. The water currents and shallow water have caused many ships to sink off this coast. That is why it is sometimes called the "Graveyard of the Atlantic."

Cape Hatteras Lighthouse is the tallest lighthouse in America. There have been three lighthouses built at this location. The current lighthouse was built around 1869. It is 208 feet (63 m) high. People can climb to the top of the lighthouse. They walk more than 250 stairs in a spiral staircase.

The First Flight

Wilbur and Orville Wright are famous brothers. Together, they invented the first flying machine that actually flew. Their airplane flew for the first time near Kitty Hawk, North Carolina. This happened on December 17, 1903.

Orville was the first one to fly. That first flight was only about 12 seconds long. The brothers flew three more times that day. Wilbur is known for the longest flight. He flew 852 feet (260 m) in about one minute. These short flights eventually changed the way people travel.

Today, people can visit the site of the Wrights' flights. The Wright Brothers National Memorial is in Kitty Hawk. Visitors can climb to the top of Kill Devil Hill to see where the airplanes took off. People can also visit a museum to learn more about the Wrights and airplanes.

To see the actual airplane the Wrights flew, people can visit the National Air and Space Museum in Washington, D.C.

The Wright Brothers National Memorial

North Carolina

1587: The 117 settlers of "The Lost Colony" arrive.

1789: North Carolina becomes the 12th state on November 21.

1792: Raleigh becomes the state capital.

1861: The American Civil War begins. North Carolina says it is no longer part of the United States.

1868: North Carolina rejoins the United States.

1903: The Wright brothers fly the first motor-powered airplane near Kitty Hawk.

1959: Research Triangle Park opens.

1989: North Carolina celebrates its bicentennial.

2002: Elizabeth Dole becomes the first female senator from North Carolina.

2003: The centennial of the Wright brothers first flight.

The Wright brothers fly near Kitty Hawk.

The Wright brothers

Cities In North Carolina

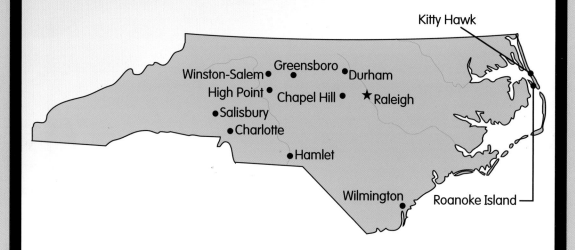

Kitty Hawk

Winston-Salem
Greensboro
Durham

High Point
Chapel Hill
★ Raleigh

Salisbury

Charlotte

Hamlet

Wilmington

Roanoke Island

Important Words

American Civil War the United States war between the Northern and Southern states.

bicentennial 200-year anniversary.

capital a city where government leaders meet.

centennial 100-year anniversary.

colony a settlement. Colonists are the people who live in a colony.

impeach to try a public official for doing wrong while serving in a public office.

nickname a name that describes something special about a person or a place.

textile having to do with cloth or fabric.

Web Sites

To learn more about North Carolina, visit ABDO Publishing Company on the World Wide Web. Web site links about North Carolina are featured on our Book Links page. These links are routinely monitored and updated to provide the most current information available.

www.abdopub.com

Index

CARROLL SCHOCHLER PRIMARY SCHOOL